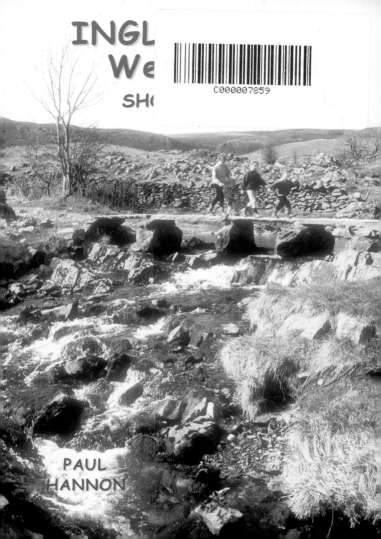

INGL...
We...
SHO...

C000007859

PAUL
HANNON

HILLSIDE PUBLICATIONS
20 Wheathead Crescent
Keighley
West Yorkshire
BD22 6LX

First Published 2010

© Paul Hannon 2010

ISBN 978 1 870141 95 6

*The sketch maps are based on 1947 OS one-inch maps
and earlier OS six-inch maps*

Cover illustration: Thornton Force, Ingleton
Back cover: Ingleborough from Twisleton
Page 1: In Crummack Dale
(Paul Hannon/Hillslides Picture Library)

Printed by Steffprint
Unit 5, Keighley Industrial Park
Royd Ings Avenue
Keighley
West Yorkshire
BD21 4DZ

CONTENTS

INTRODUCTION

Ingleton sits at the south-western corner of the Yorkshire Dales, an area dominated by spectacular limestone landscapes beneath sweeping mountains. Ingleborough, Whernside and Gragareth are regular backdrops to most scenes in the district: along their flanks is an array of gleaming scars and pavements, gaping potholes and labyrinthine caves all of which are fascinating to seek out and explore. Mighty Ingleborough dominates the eastern half of this area, while the River Lune forms the western limit. The Lune rises on the Howgill Fells, and en route to the scenic market town of Kirkby Lonsdale it neatly marks the western limit of the Dales, flowing between the rolling country of Middleton and Casterton Fells on its east bank and unfrequented parkland to the west.

In this richly diverse area you can move easily from bracing fellwalk to riverside ramble. The village of Clapham is rightly a dales magnet, and the area around here and Austwick is one of the best pockets of walking country in the land. By contrast, the little-known Barbon district is an unsung gem. Amid this wonderful scenery is the unique collection of waterfalls on the edge of Ingleton itself. Variety of surroundings is equalled by variety of location, as North Yorkshire is joined by Cumbria and Lancashire.

Kirkby Lonsdale is a delightful little town high above the River Lune. From the market square streets of shops, pubs and cafes radiate. The church of St Mary the Virgin dates from the 12th century, and boasts excellent views, as an octagonal gazebo looks out over the Lune. Turner painted this view and Ruskin enthused over it: a path lets you do likewise en route to the town's best known feature, Devil's Bridge.

The majority of walks are on rights of way with no access restrictions. Some also make use of 'Right to Roam' to cross Open Country, and on most days of the year you are free to walk responsibly over these wonderful areas. Of various restrictions, two most notable are that dogs are normally banned from grouse moors; and that the areas can be closed for up to 28 days each year, subject to advance notice. The Countryside Agency and information centres have more details. Whilst the route description should be sufficient to guide you around, a map is recommended for greater information: Ordnance Survey 1:25,000 scale maps give the finest detail, and Explorer OL2 covers all of the walks, with just one overlapping onto OL41.

Whernside from Southerscales

USEFUL INFORMATION

·Yorkshire Dales National Park (01756-752748)
·Ingleton Tourist Information (015242-41049)
·Settle Tourist Information (01729-825192)
·Horton Tourist Information (01729-860333)
·Kendal Tourist Information (01539-725758)
·Yorkshire Dales Society (01729-825600)
·Open Access (0845-100 3298) www.countrysideaccess.gov.uk
·Traveline - public transport information (0870-6082608)

INGLETON
& the Western Dales

20 Short Scenic Walks

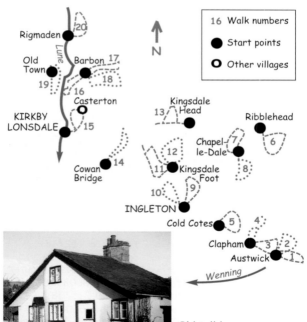

16	Walk numbers
●	Start points
O	Other villages

N ↑

Rigmaden 20

Old Town

Lune

Barbon 17

19

16 Casterton

18

KIRKBY LONSDALE 1 15

Cowan Bridge 14

Kingsdale Head

13

Chapel-le-Dale 7

Ribblehead

6

12

11 Kingsdale Foot

8

10 9

INGLETON

Cold Cotes 5

4

Clapham 3 2

Austwick 1

Wenning

Old toll house, Casterton

A RECORD OF YOUR WALKS

WALK	DATE	NOTES
1		
2		
3		
4		
5		
6		
7		
8		
9		
10		
11		
12		
13		
14		
15		
16		
17		
18		
19		
20		

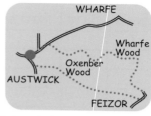

*3¾ miles
from Austwick*

**Some delectable natural
woodland amid idyllic
limestone surroundings**

*Start Village centre (GR:
767684), roadside parking
Map OS Explorer OL2, Yorkshire Dales South/West
Explorer OL41, Forest of Bowland & Ribblesdale (tiny part)
Access Open Access, see page 5*

From the green outside the Gamecock Inn turn down the narrow lane opposite, and quickly take a snicket on the right. Past the houses it emerges as a flagged path through two fields to join a road on the village edge. Turn left to Austwick Bridge, with a good view to Moughton's flat top. Across, turn left on Wood Lane, a walled track. Where it bends left leave by a gate/stile on the right to cross a long field to a stile onto a walled bridleway to the right of Wood House. Cross straight over to climb a field to a stile on the brow. Pausing to appraise the view, Austwick nestles beneath the flat top of Ingleborough, its sidekick Simon Fell also well seen: Robin Proctor's Scar projects beneath Norber and its boulder-field, while ahead, Feizor is revealed beneath Pot Scar.

From the stile begin a march through a string of stiles in this block of fields with Oxenber and Feizor Woods on the left. In spring a riot of primroses fill the base of this limestone woodland. Stiles come thick and fast towards the end, maintaining a near-straight line to enter Feizor across a tiny beck. This is an unspoilt settlement in a hollow in the hills served only by a cul-de-sac. Note the setted watersplash across the street with troughs alongside, and a café to the left. Go left to the terminus of the road at the end of the village, where a waterpump and trough sit outside a row of cottages. Swinging left in front of them an unsurfaced road climbs away, alongside Feizor Wood to the gap of Feizor Nick.

A supreme moment comes on the crest as Penyghent appears ahead. Passing through a gate, within yards take a stile left into Wharfe Wood's Open Access land. A path meanders away through scrubby trees, soon swinging left up to a clearing on a knoll. Here it bears right to run close by a wall on the left. With intermittent views out to Ingleborough the path gently declines into denser trees to arrive at a corner wall-stile. This puts you into Oxenber Wood, and the path drops into more open surrounds. Soon swinging left it rises gently to run through largely open terrain amid scattered limestone. Soon entering a vast, flat clearing, a junction of the two main paths is reached. Double back right, soon descending colourful pasture.

Ahead is Wharfe beneath Moughton, with Ingleborough dominant beyond. Swinging right to drop towards a clump of trees, the path then swings left beneath it and down through bracken to a path and intake wall along the base. Go left through a gate/stile, and the green path drops down with the wall to drop to a gate/stile at the bottom. Leaving Open Access land, a short walled path drops down onto another walled way, Wood Lane again. Just a few yards left take a stile on the right and descend the field to a stile at the very bottom. This puts you onto a walled bridleway. Turn right to a ford at Flascoe Bridge: this clapper bridge on Austwick Beck gives a splendid final moment. Across, the way soon broadens out and runs on to the road on the edge of the village, going left to finish.

The path through Oxenber Wood

*4¼ miles
from Austwick*

**Supremely easy walking
amid some truly beautiful
Dales limestone scenery**

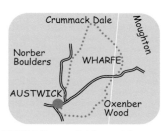

*Start Village centre (GR: 767684), roadside parking
Map OS Explorer OL2, Yorkshire Dales South/West*

Austwick is an attractive village set well back from the main A65 road. A small green, the cosy Gamecock Inn, an old hall, shop and countless tidy cottages combine to create a picture of great charm. The tiny church of the Epiphany with its little bell-cote sits at the green junction. From the green outside the pub head east out of the village, away from the centre. Passing a 1673 datestone on a two-storey gabled porch on the right, Moughton's flat top is quickly revealed ahead.

Beyond the last houses an enclosed bridleway turns off right to reach Flascoe Bridge and a ford on Austwick Beck. This is a charming spot as you cross the first of the day's two clapper bridges. Continuing, almost at once take a stile on the left into a field. Rise to a stile in the top left corner to join another enclosed way, Wood Lane. Turn left on its lovely course, broadening out to run along by Wood End Farm and out onto a road. Go right for a couple of minutes then turn left by a barn up an enclosed old lane (a bridleway) that ascends gently into the hamlet of Wharfe. Moughton offers a colourful and arresting profile above.

Rise straight on between the houses to a junction. Going left for a few yards you then turn up a track right, though first continue a few strides further left to see the lovely Manor House of 1715. Wharfe is an improbable chocolate box hamlet, hidden from the outside world by leafy lanes that function only as bridle-ways to the public. Back at the track it immediately climbs out of the hamlet, as White Stone Lane. High above you are the gleaming limestone scars that seam Moughton's flanks, though sections of your enclosing walls are composed of the very different Silurian rock that is exposed across some of the fields. The old lane runs a splendid course into Crummack Dale to ultimately arrive at a fork: bear left down to a superb clapper bridge and ford on Austwick Beck. This is a grand spot to linger, complete with a seat.

Very shortly after crossing take a small gateway on the left and cross a stile into the field behind. Rise directly up past scattered Silurian rocks to a stile on the brow: pause to look back over the great stretch of Crummack Dale framed between Norber and Moughton. A faint green way descends a large stony field to Sowerthwaite Farm drive. Cross to a stile behind, and from the next one advance to the near wall corner, with Crummack Lane just over it. Leaving the wallside, drop down to a stream and a stile by a barn then rise to a corner stile onto a rough lane. Cross straight over and down the wallside to a stile into a garden. The way runs straight down between houses out onto Townhead Lane. Turn down to the bottom and go right for the village centre.

The Manor House, Wharfe

4¾ miles from Clapham

Easy rambling to a famous collection of alien boulders and a lovely village

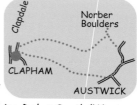

Start Village centre (GR: 745692), National Park car park
Map OS Explorer OL2, Yorkshire Dales South/West
Access Open Access, see page 5

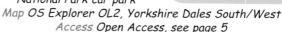

Clapham is a beautiful village at the foot of Ingleborough, from where Clapham Beck flows to form the centrepiece. Several attractive bridges are in evidence, and a splendid array of cottages line the parallel lane. Centrally placed are the New Inn, Post office, shops and cafes. By the car park/WC is the Manor House with a 1705 lintel, and the Cave Rescue Organisation HQ. Just up the road is the church of St James with a 15th century tower. For many decades, into the 1990s, Clapham provided the cottage home for that revered Yorkshire magazine the Dalesman.

From the car park head up the road towards the church on the south side of the beck. Bear right outside the churchyard, as a bridleway takes over to pass beneath tunnels built by the Farrar family for access from the hall over the lane to their surrounding grounds. It rises initially steeply through woodland to the junction of Thwaite Lane and Long Lane. Keep straight on for some time, with Ingleborough appearing back over to the left. After a slight dip take a stile on the left, from where a faint path crosses to the right of the marshy site of a tarn. Ahead is the imposing cliff of Robin Proctor's Scar, a popular climbing ground: keep right to a wall corner, following it to a corner stile beneath the scar. In Open Country advance on with the wall on your right to reach a fork: that dropping with the wall is your onward route, but for now rise left to a guidepost at a path crossroads on a little shelf amid scattered Silurian rocks: you are now just beneath the Norber boulderfield. Turn left, squeezing up between limestone outcrops to a prominent large cairn on a pile of stones. You are now on the plateau on which the boulders rest, largely along to the right: time to explore!

The Norber Boulders are geological freaks, intriguing specimens of something the Ice Age brought in. A retreating glacier carried rocks from further up Crummack Dale and deposited them in their present position. What is so special is that they are dark Silurian rocks atop white limestone pedestals that have worn more rapidly away. They are termed 'erratic', and are a bit special. Back at the guidepost drop onto the lower path, which traces the wall down to a stile by a small gate at the bottom to leave Open Country. Descend the fieldside, and part way along bear left to a gate/stile near the corner. Rejoining Thwaite Lane, go left a few steps to a crossroads with Crummack Lane, and turn right to descend into Austwick. At the bottom turn right into the centre, soon reaching the Gamecock Inn. For a note on Austwick see page 10.

Continue past the pub to the green outside the shop, and keep right until reaching a gate/stile on the right between houses. Accessing a field corner a broad grassy way slants up the field, crossing to a wall-stile and along to another, behind which is a spring. Throughout this return you have big views over the Wenning Valley to Bowland. The path rises above a small wood to maintain a superb, simple line through the fields, the latter stages seeing old iron kissing-gates replacing the stiles. Joining a farm track, the path runs a parallel course to its right, avoiding the farmyard and at the end running as a snicket alongside the car park to finish.

At the Norber Boulders

13

4¹2 miles from Clapham

The absorbing valley of Clapdale leads to an impressive limestone ravine

Start Village centre (GR: 745692),
National Park car park
Map OS Explorer OL2,
Yorkshire Dales South/West
Access Opening section is on private
land with small entry fee to Ingleborough estate

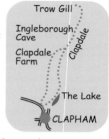

For a note on Clapham see page 12. From the car park cross the road to a characterful stone-arched footbridge and take the road to the right. Note an impressive waterfall plunging under an arched bridge in the estate grounds. As the road turns left, pass through a gateway in front where a ticket machine collects modest dues for entering the private grounds. A broad path zigzags up to quickly reach the foot of a surprisingly extensive ornamental lake, locked in glorious woodland created by the Farrer family of Ingleborough Hall in the 19th century. Reginald Farrer (1880-1920) found fame as a botanist, collecting alpine plants on journeys to far-flung parts and bringing many back to the hall grounds. The broad carriageway is followed the length of the charming estate grounds: part way on is an old yew embedded with hundreds of coins.

The drive climbs away from the lake, a sustained pull high above the tumbling beck to reach the Grotto. A short way beyond, you emerge into the open air of the upper reaches of Clapdale. With Norber's flanks up to the right, the drive traces Clapham Beck to Ingleborough Cave. This is a showcave with guided tours: hot drinks are available. Just yards past it a stone-arched bridge crosses the beck within yards of its birth. On the left is Beck Head, from where the waters gush. The stream last saw daylight as Fell Beck, plunging into Gaping Gill high on the moor above. A connection by cavers was only established in the 1980s after many years' efforts.

Over the bridge pass through a gate/stile and along a dry trough between low limestone scars. On the bend, set back on the left at the base of a cliff is Foxholes, a small cave that has revealed evidence of New Stone Age occupation. The corner is rounded to reveal Trow Gill just ahead, and your path climbs into it. This former cave is now an overhanging ravine, Gordale in style if not in proportions: unlike Gordale Scar its valley is dry, but it's still a grand place to be. Retrace steps to Ingleborough Cave, and back along the carriageway until approaching the woods. A hundred yards before the gate take a gate/stile on the right, from where a broad path slants up the flank, climbing to Clapdale Farm. At the rear turn left through a gate/stile into its yard, then head away along its rough access road through the fields. This gives good views across Clapdale to the broad plateau of Norber, with the Bowland moors ahead. Descending to become enclosed and later surfaced, it drops down to emerge onto a back road in the village: go left to finish, concluding by crossing the first bridge to approach the church, then turning right for the car park.

Trow Gill

*3½ miles
from Cold Cotes*

**A gentle climb to inviting
moorland to discover
potholes and pavements
in Ingleborough's shadow**

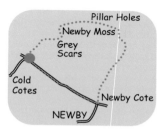

*Start Old road above hamlet (GR: 719714), roadside parking
100 yards east of junction at foot of common
Map OS Explorer OL2, Yorkshire Dales South/West
Access Open Access, see page 5*

The walk begins with a mile-long stroll on the quiet road towards Clapham, the original road linking it with Ingleton. Almost at once a Clapham-Ingleton boundary stone is passed in a little dip. It descends gently with big views across the Wenning Valley to the Bowland moors. The road is followed as far as the hamlet of Newby Cote, at a junction with a road climbing from Newby. Turn left up the track past the nearest buildings, rising as a grassy walled way past an old quarry to a gate/stile onto the open moor. Though the track bears off right, remain by the wall up to its corner, noting an old limekiln just over it.

A path rises half-left up the grassy moor to a hollowed, grassed over small quarry just above. It keeps straight up its left side and a lovely little path now remains underfoot for all of the climb. Initially straight, it soon starts to bear generally right. Before long Penyghent appears to the right, and on a little rise by some mixed rocks, Little Ingleborough looms directly above. Your way angles further right, contouring to pass between low limestone scars and two minutes further to a cairn. Here turn off across pathless grassy moor to a prominent characterful boulder on the left, with the distinctive Harryhorse Stone a little beyond. Ingleborough's flat summit now appears beyond Little Ingleborough's dome.

A fading trod points the way right, slightly uphill for five minutes further, passing various sinkholes to reach a massive one. Here strike left, immediately crossing Grey Wife Sike: intermittent trods lead along an endless line of sinkholes. Maintain a level course as slopes rise gently to the right, while further left is the limestone shelf of Grey Scars. Keep a slightly higher line to locate the impressive Fluted Hole. Some 150 yards further is a superb chain of holes bedecked with rowans: finest of these shafts is Pillar Holes. Another 150 yards across slightly moister ground is mighty Long Kin West Pot amid a cluster of lesser holes. The main shaft falls a sheer 300ft/90m, with a total depth of around 550ft/168m.

Your return begins on a well-defined sunken way slanting gently away, reedy but with a thin trod alongside. Reaching further sinkholes ignore those contouring on still further, and remain on the improving way to slant down to the far end of Grey Scars, where it meets a broader grass track. This leads unfailingly down to Cold Cotes, but consider a short loop left up onto Grey Scars. The scattered limestone pavement is crossed to two prominent cairns, with an 'erratic' 'I/N' (Ingleton/Newby) boundary stone alongside. Instead of a direct return to the track you could slant down easy slopes to pick up the descent route. Conclude down this grassy way, savouring big views across to Bowland's moors. The track finishes as a broad way through dry reeds, deflected by sheep pens to a gate onto an access road just yards above your starting point.

*Harryhorse Stone, looking
to Little Ingleborough*

4 miles
from Ribblehead

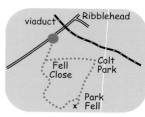

A simple ascent of the northernmost summit of the Ingleborough massif

Start *Ingleton road*
(GR: 760788), large lay-by half-mile from junction
Map *OS Explorer OL2, Yorkshire Dales South/West*
Access *Open Access (entire walk), see page 5*

Ribblehead stands where the Ribblesdale and Ingleton-Hawes roads meet: only buildings are the Station Inn and railway cottages. The railway earned national fame in the shape of 24-arch Batty Moss Viaduct, the symbol of Victorian enterprise that became the symbol of a successful campaign to prevent closure of the line in the 1980s. All the Three Peaks are well seen at various stages: mighty Whernside throughout, Ingleborough offers its most shapely side for much of the walk, while Penyghent is also well seen.

From the Ingleton end of the lay-by a roadside gate sends a grassy track away past a low scar before doubling back left to head away near the wall. Park Fell, Simon Fell and Ingleborough form a stepped skyline ahead, while there is a brief early sighting of Penyghent. The track is soon deflected right by limestone: leave its faltering course by bearing right to trace a distinct boundary between limestone turf and acidic grasses, crossing to a gate in the wall opposite. An improving green track heads away across Sleights Pasture to quickly fork. Bear left through a low limestone scar, becoming briefly faint but reforming, past an outer wall corner and along towards a wall ahead. Before reaching it a firmer track is met: go left on this past pens to a gate in the intake wall ahead.

Remain on the track heading away, leaving limestone country and swinging right. After a slight rise it runs a level course along the foot of the moor, lined by sinkholes. Approaching a wall it swings left, slanting up to approach it, crossing a tiny stream to climb near the wall. As a fence takes over the track fades, and steep but easy ground sees you up the final haul. On the crest a wall appears, and the 'ridge' path is joined. With climbing accomplished turn left, the path tracing the wall along with massive views over Ribblehead to Whernside, back to Ingleborough and all around this corner of the Dales. The wall leads to a junction where your onward route is the path straight ahead with old wall and fence, but from a stile and gate a path first doubles back two minutes up to visit the waiting Ordnance Survey column. At 1847ft/563m Park Fell is the northernmost outpost of the Ingleborough massif, making a recognisable domed landmark around the Ribblehead area.

Back at the wall corner resume on the main path north, commencing a rapid descent towards a wild Ribblehead panorama. The path follows the fence down to a stile at the bottom corner. Continue down towards Colt House, just yards before which double back left on a thinner path to a wall-stile. Head directly away on a level stroll to a bridle-gate. A little further is another one in the wall to the right, defended by Fell Close Rocks. A path bears away to a ladder-stile ahead. Scattered around and on your right are the contorted shapes of Sleights Pasture Rocks. Over the stile follow the wall right to the corner passed early in the walk. Bear right from it to rejoin the outward track, crossing the low limestone band and bearing right to the second gate of the walk, crossing the final pasture as you began, back to the roadside gate.

Park Fell, looking to Ingleborough

4 miles
from Chapel-le-Dale

Easy walking through a fascinating area between Ingleborough and Whernside

Start Hill Inn (GR: 742776), with lay-bys above pub
Map OS Explorer OL2, Yorkshire Dales South/West

Chapel-le-Dale is a scattered community on and around the Ingleton-Ribblehead road. The Hill Inn (properly the 'Old Hill') stands in isolation with 'the hill', Ingleborough, rising spectacularly behind. From the pub head south along the Ingleton road. From the outset Ingleborough forms an awesome profile ahead above limestone tiers. Within minutes turn right on a road deep into trees, and St Leonard's hidden church. It was restored in 1869, though some mullioned windows remain. Buried here were scores of victims from railway construction days at Ribblehead - killed by disease. Fork right again here up an inviting lane: immersed in greenery on the right are Hurtle Pot (right by the road), Jingle Pot and Weathercote Cave. Ignoring a private branch left, the road becomes rougher to wind up past Gill Head. Its journey is sheer delight: an odd feature is a modern statue en route, a plaque explains. Gill Head, dated 1607, boasts an Arcadian setting.

The road quickly emerges onto open moorland with the broad shoulders of Whernside dominant. As the way runs on across this large moorland pasture to approach Ellerbeck, Ribblehead Viaduct appears and remains in sight for much of the walk. The track swings right to run to the farm, and Whernside is seen at its shapeliest from this point. Pass along the front of the house into the yard, and out via gates to the right. A broad track heads off across the field and then beneath limestone scars to Bruntscar.

All the way from Ellerbeck to Broadrake the route runs beneath a low, wooded limestone scar. A string of farms make use of its shelter and the springs that rise from its base. Just beyond the buildings at Bruntscar, alongside an old kiln the farm road turns right to some modern barns: ignore this and advance to a small gate by a barn ahead. A grass track crosses the next pasture to Broadrake Farm, where turn right down the drive. As it goes right and crosses a cattle-grid, bear left on a grassy track over rough pasture. At an early fork go left to a gate/stile. The green track then heads away to ford normally dry Winterscales Beck. If not dry, turn briefly downstream to where it should sink below ground at Gatekirk Sinks. Across, it curves less clearly right to join a surfaced road.

Turn right and leave the road immediately after a cattle-grid, a path following the wall to a bridle-gate in the corner on the right. With Gatekirk Cave enclosed in trees to the right, follow the left-hand wall away, and when it departs keep on to the far end, where the mischievous beck can at times sink emphatically under-ground. Cross the dry bed to a gate behind: on your left is the deep, tree-lined bowl of Haws Gill Wheel. Here waters spring up only to immediately pour in and sink below ground again. From another gate just in front, follow the wall away through a field, and at a gate an enclosed way (the natural line of the beck) leads to a farm road. Follow it left, past Philpin (refreshments in season) and onto the main road just below the pub.

Chapel-le-Dale church

*2³⁴ miles
from Chapel-le-Dale*

**A near-level stroll visiting
absorbing limestone features
in Ingleborough's shadow**

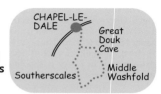

CHAPEL-LE-
DALE

Great
Douk
Cave

Southerscales

Middle
Washfold

*Start Hill Inn (GR: 742776), with lay-bys above pub
Map OS Explorer OL2, Yorkshire Dales South/West
Access Open Access, see page 5*

This walk is dominated by mighty Ingleborough, most famous mountain in the Pennines, and nowhere does it asserts itself more than above Chapel-le-Dale, a scattered community on and around the Ingleton-Ribblehead road. The Hill Inn (properly the 'Old Hill') stands in isolation with 'the hill', Ingleborough, rising spectacularly behind. The pub is immensely popular with hillwalkers and cavers, while the old school serves as a bunkhouse. St Leonard's tiny church is all but hidden in a cradle of foliage. Restored in 1869, some lovely mullioned windows remain. It also has an attractive little bell turret. Buried here were scores of victims from railway construction days at Ribblehead - killed by disease.

From the pub head up the road for 100 yards to a stile on the right, and rise to join the bridleway as it approaches a gate. Or, from the lay-bys above, drop towards the pub and take a gate on the left. Immediately, Ingleborough's majestic stance fires the spirits, and a panel provides information on Ingleborough National Nature Reserve. A good track winds away past a well-preserved limekiln, bound directly for the mountain. Through a gate a much gentler green way continues straight on through two further gates in walls between lush limestone pastures. You enter Southerscales Nature Reserve, owned by the Yorkshire Wildlife Trust. This first mile gives ample time to appraise the layout of this side of the mountain. After a branch to Great Douk Cave goes left, a firmer track re-forms. Rising gently beneath a limestone scar, it swings left up to cross the edge of the Southerscales pavement. The track runs on past the massive sinkhole of Braithwaite Wife Hole to a pair of stiles onto the fell proper. This marks a very sudden transition from limestone pastures to more austere, brown fellside.

Eschewing the mountain-bound stone-flagged path that now takes over, instead turn left on a lesser path that runs above the wall all the way along the moor-foot to the far end. Faced with two stiles take that in the wall ahead, from where a path crosses towards limestone outcrops at Middle Washfold Cave. Here a small pavement and a solitary tree decorate the hole, which after rain swallows a sizeable stream. Alongside is an old stone sheepfold, while Ingleborough, inevitably, makes a fine backdrop.

The path curves left in front of Middle Washfold, then on to a gate in a wall. Continuing away, it bears right to approach the environs of Great Douk Cave, enclosed by a sturdy wall. On the right just before it is the sinister-looking shaft of Little Douk Pot, accessed by a stile. Curve round the outside of Great Douk's wall and go left to the bottom, where a stile gives access. A rough path drops into the massive hollow bedecked in trees. At the top end a waterspout gushes enthusiastically out, to quickly seep innocuously below ground again. Alongside is the vertical, covered shaft of Great Douk Pot with fixed ladders descending eerily into the bowels of the earth. Re-emerging, a broad way drops down to rapidly rejoin the outward route just a couple of fields from the start.

Whernside from Southerscales

4½ miles
from Ingleton

**A classic walk visiting
a series of waterfalls
in twin wooded gorges**

*Start Village centre
(GR: 693732), Falls car park
Map OS Explorer OL2, Yorkshire Dales South/West
Access Much of walk is over private land,
and requires payment at start (parking included)*

Commonly known as the Waterfalls Walk, this is one of two famous excursions from Ingleton, the other being an ascent of its hill, Ingleborough. The falls walk has attracted visitors for over a century, and more so than most, it is worth savouring in one of the winter months when free of jostling crowds. The paths are well maintained everywhere - justifying the charge - but care is needed when wet leaves carpet the ground. Be also aware that for a low-level walk, there is a fair amount of 'up and down' work. The two valleys explored on this walk are remarkably alike, each beautifully wooded and exposing some fascinating geological features, with the Craven Faults much in evidence. For some reason the names of the watercourses have caused confusion: the Twiss is known by some as the Greta, while more curiously Wainwright transposed the Greta (Twiss) and the Doe. What is less in doubt is that at their meeting, if not any earlier, the Greta is born.

The village of Ingleton is at the heart of Yorkshire's limestone country, and is an ideal base for exploring the fells, scars, caves and valleys. The centre is dominated by a viaduct on the former Clapham-Tebay line. Also prominent is St Mary's church, while there are a number of interesting little corners. There is a youth hostel, numerous pubs, cafes and shops, and even a climbing wall and a swimming pool should you require a change of activity.

Few directions are needed as the paths are very clear throughout, and the way is obvious. From the car park the path heads up the valley of the Twiss, twice crossing the river above Swilla Glen to arrive at Pecca Falls. More open country follows, passing a former refreshment hut to reach the walk's highlight at Thornton Force. Few will not take a sojourn here. Above it, another bridge takes the path up to Twisleton Lane. Above Thornton Force lies the flat valley floor of Kingsdale, at one time a glacial lake held back by the moraine of Raven Ray. Turn right on its green course, becoming surfaced on dropping down to Twisleton Hall. Here bear left on a track passing above all the buildings, on through a gate/stile at the end. A good path crosses the field and descends to a gate onto a back road. Fine views to Ingleborough dominate this section.

Go straight across to Beezleys Farm, on between the buildings to a gate on the left. Drop down to Beezley Falls and follow the River Doe back downstream. Features along the way include a viewing platform above the Baxengill Gorge, the Snow Falls, and one crossing of the beck. Emergence from the trees is high above the river at Cat Leap Fall. The path runs to a road-end to re-enter the village. The final section has an interesting prospect of tilted rock strata in the old quarry across the river.

Pecca Falls

*3½ miles
from Ingleton*

**Simple rambling on
unassuming paths to
a lovely little village**

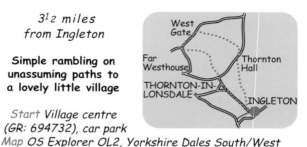

Start Village centre
(GR: 694732), car park
Map OS Explorer OL2, Yorkshire Dales South/West

For a note on Ingleton see page 24. From the church on the main street descend the side road to bridge the River Greta, with the Waterfalls car park just beyond. While the mighty viaduct dominates the scene, the remains of an old railway bridge are also visible to the right: this was a tiny branch that served a quarry. Don't enter but take a stile in front and a firm path ascends into unkempt pasture. A path bears right across to a cutting of the aforementioned quarry branch. Behind is a kissing-gate, from which follow the sturdy wall away. The limestone scars of Hunt's Cross rise ahead, Ingleborough's classic frame is over to the right, with Thornton's church tower to the left. Encountering kissing-gate, barn and spring, remain with the wall until it bends right to a corner stile. Ascend a large field towards Thornton Hall, passing a fence corner to a neat wall-stile by a barn. Rise up the enclosure side onto the drive at the farm, with Thornton Lane just to the left. Opposite is Glebe Farm with its big square chimney.

Ascend the road for two minutes to the next house, and take a short enclosed way in front of its garden. Emerging into a field bear right to a gate/stile at the far corner. Over to the left is a long Bowland skyline. Advance to a gate/stile into the remains of Cowgill Farm. From the stile look down the field to see an old burial mound left of a clump of trees. Pass between the buildings to another gate/stile alongside the surviving privy, and on over a stream above a wooded gill. Head away, merging with a wall on the right to reach a corner stile. Maintain this line, on above a newly planted wood and on again to a stile onto the sunken Westgate Lane. Go left past West Gate Farm down to a junction alongside another farm: here go left on a side road. After a minute leave by a stile on the left, through a tiny enclosure then away with a wall on your right: Ingleborough is majestic ahead. From a plank bridge and wall-stile at the end, advance a little further to a stile in a kink at the wall-end. Resume on the other side, tracing a hedge to a ladder-stile, where Thornton's church re-appears down to the right. Drop down this field towards the far end, and take the right-hand ladder-stile. Head towards Thornton, but not to the far end, instead bear right to a gate in the hedge ahead. Follow a line of trees away then swing left to a gate onto a junction alongside church and pub.

Thornton-in-Lonsdale is little more than a hamlet, yet boasts the two staple elements of a real village as pub and church sit opposite each other. St Oswald's has a sturdy tower, while the Marton Arms is an enterprising hostelry with a 1679 datestone above the door. War memorial, Victorian postbox, phone box and stocks also reside on or around the junction. To finish simply follow the road straight ahead, keeping left at a fork after bridging the old railway, and left again to drop gently down, with a footway, to the old viaduct in Ingleton, passing beneath it to conclude.

The Marton Arms, Thornton-in-Lonsdale

*4¹₂ miles
from Kingsdale Foot*

**Clear tracks and lanes offer
the simplest of navigation
through some splendid
limestone surrounds**

*Start Kingsdale (GR: 691756), 1¹₂ miles on Dent road out
of Thornton-in-Lonsdale: lay-by at end of old quarry on brow
Map OS Explorer OL2, Yorkshire Dales South/West
Access Open access, see page 5*

     Kingsdale is a classic glaciated valley: uniform scars seam
the walls of the dale, and a moraine at its foot suggests a lake once
occupied the dale floor. From the outset Ingleborough's majestic form
dominates the scene back over the valley, while Whernside rises up
Kingsdale. Enter Open Access land through a gate by the lay-by with
a small stone hut ahead, and a grassy track rises left towards the
wall, then makes a longer slant right before doubling back towards
the wall. The way settles down to a steady rise close by the wall, with
limestone outcrops on your right. Passing through a gate in a wall
ahead, the main way slants right to rise to a pronounced skyline nick.
To your left is Tow Scar's Ordnance Survey column at 1256ft/383m.
     Ahead is the big limestone knoll of North End Scar,
deflecting the track right to rise delightfully through an amphitheatre
between limestone outcrops. At the top it emerges onto the open
moor of Low Plain, with Gragareth's slopes high ahead: this is the fell
on which your entire route is walked. The way swings left and the
outcrops recede as it runs a mercurial, near-level course across to a
wall. On joining it at a small cairn the good track of the Turbary Road
is found to run alongside it. Turbary is the right of commoners to dig
peat for fuel, and the road was constructed for the passage of carts
to Turbary Pasture higher up the fell: Walk 12 makes good use of it.

Your way turns left, and when the wall turns off remain on the track which slants down to a gate in the bottom corner. Leaving Open Country the way descends a stony, enclosed course. Within a few strides a wall-stile on the right offers a chance to visit Marble Steps Pot, its location identified by the crown of a large cluster of trees back up on the moor. An initially flagged path heads away, only to fade in miry ground. A little further your path forks right off the main one at a sinkhole, and rises to the left of two massive sinkholes to arrive at Marble Steps Pot. This massive hole is quite a spectacle, with a total depth of some 425ft/130m: take care!

Back on the stony lane it descends with big views across to a long skyline of the Bowland moors to shortly reach a junction. Alongside is a water treatment works, with the head of surfaced Masongill Fell Lane dropping away. Your route is the more inviting left branch, Tow Scar Road. This nicely surfaced green lane runs an unerring course for a considerable time. En route you pass beneath the scars of Tow Scar and Hunt's Cross, the central section being open along a fieldside. On becoming enclosed again it rises up to a minor brow to reveal Ingleborough ahead. The lane then curves down to the right to drop onto a road at a seat. Turn left, rising past a radio station to reach a junction with the Kingsdale road. A view indicator stands alongside some seats, but don't expect to see everything that's on it! A short further rise will return you to the start.

Kingsdale, looking to Whernside

4¾ miles from Kingsdale Foot

A classic glaciated valley with outstanding limestone features

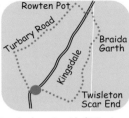

Start Kingsdale (GR: 692759), 1¾ miles on Dent road out of Thornton-in-Lonsdale: verge parking by Twisleton Lane
Map OS Explorer OL2, Yorkshire Dales South/West
Access Open access, see page 5

From the Twisleton Lane junction head a few yards back towards Thornton to a stile on the right. A thin trod climbs to one on the skyline, clambering through limestone outcrops at the top. Part way up, Ingleborough's majestic form appears back over the valley. Initially curving left, the way climbs through more outcrops to rise to a shelf with old sheepfolds to your right. Up the small gully behind, the outcrops recede as you emerge onto open pasture with Gragareth ahead. Take a trod inclining half-right over gentler ground to close in on a sturdy wall, rising steadily but not actually meeting it until the top corner. Here you meet the Turbary Road at a wall junction.

Turn through the gate and head off along this superb old track. The only thing to concentrate on is ensuring most of the caves in the vicinity are seen: some can't be missed. Turbary is the right of commoners to dig peat for fuel, and the road was constructed for the passage of carts to the Turbary Pasture. Today it is a splendid walkers' way along a limestone shelf, offering a grand prospect of Whernside and is a perfect springboard for inspection of a series of caves and holes. Through the first gate Kail Pot is 25 yards off-track in a grassy hollow: this deep drop is the only one safely fenced. Through a gate ahead, ignore a branch curving right to another gate. A parallel wall shadows you to the next gate. Very quickly you reach the dry bed of a tiny stream, leading 150 yards left to Swinsto Hole. This unassuming entrance to an important cave system is found just to the right. Slant back to Turbary Pot, a distinctive hole by the track.

Beyond a further gate it's quickly on to the visual feast of Rowten Pot, appearing suddenly by the path. Draped in vegetation, the gaping chasm drops some 350ft/107m: adjacent is a less obvious, more sinister hole. Across the path is the collapsed roof of Rowten Cave, its entrance 100 yards up the moor. Don't use the gate behind, but make use of Open Access to turn down the near side of the wall: Braida Garth appears across the valley as you drop by low scars. Towards the bottom veer away from the wall to a gate onto the road. Go briefly left, a stile on the right accessing a footbridge on the stony bed of Kingsdale Beck: this normally subterranean stream re-surfaces at Keld Head, in between your crossings of it. Heading for the farm of Braida Garth bear left to a prominent knoll, on which is a stile in the wall. A green track then passes a modern barn to join the drive. Go left towards the house but take a small gate on the right beneath it, crossing a small enclosure to a stile into a field beneath Braida Garth Wood. Cross this field and the next to a stile beneath the end of the wood. Over it is an old limekiln, and the start of a limestone scar above.

A path slants up through dry reeds to a stile ahead (ignore a higher bridle-gate), then heads away alongside a wall. After a fence takes over and approaches a reedy tract, the path bears left across rough pasture to the next stile ahead. Continue to rise alongside a fence through the saddle ahead, with Wackenburgh Hill to the right. After stiles in successive walls a superior green track is joined to drop to the cart track of Twisleton Lane, though a more direct short-cut is possible with care. Go right on the lane, becoming enclosed to run via a footbridge and ford on Kingsdale Beck back to the start point.

Rowten Pot

*3¹2 miles
from Kingsdale Head*

**An uncomplicated ascent
of a 2000-foot fell:
save it for a clear day!**

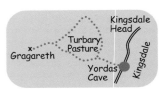

Start Yordas Cave (GR: 706790),
roadside parking half-mile south of farm
Map OS Explorer OL2, Yorkshire Dales South/West
Access Open Access (entire walk), see page 5

Embowered in trees, Yordas Cave was a 19th century showcave. A gate on the west side of the road opposite the lay-by points you up the wallside to the casual explorer's entrance, a man-made arch on the left at the foot of the gorge. Armed with a good torch it is possible to venture with care into the main chamber, known as the Great Hall. Going right to the Chapter House, a waterfall and beautiful formations are revealed. The walk proper begins by passing up to the right above the entrance and then up above the ravine to the top, crossing the beck to where it sinks underground. To the left, above, is the fenced enclosure of the entry point, Yordas Pot.

From a gateway/gap above rise up the wallside, with the beck on its other side. By now Ingleborough is already on view across Kingsdale, while the bulk of Whernside across the valley has been very evident from the outset. A trod rises to a gate in a wall junction at the top, to which you will return. Bear left over moist ground to an ascending wall, and simply follow it up to the skyline. The terrain becomes drier as things steepen above an old sheep-fold, and the final pull sees a trod wind between rocks to suddenly flatten out as Great Coum appears northwards along this long ridge. A short stroll along the wallside lead to a junction with the ridge-wall: here the Lakeland Fells appear ahead. From the stile the Ordnance Survey column is seen across to the left, and a good green path makes a five-minute crossing to it past some nice pools.

At 2057ft/627m this is the only mountain in modern Lancashire, though traditionalists will rightly point out the mighty Coniston Fells are in true Lancashire. Though connected to higher ground by a broad ridge running north to Great Coum, its position on the edge of the Yorkshire Dales renders it an extensive viewpoint. Features on show, clockwise, include the South Pennines, Pendle Hill, the Bowland moors, Morecambe Bay, the Lune Valley, Whitbarrow, Hutton Roof Crags, Farleton Fell, Black Combe, Casterton Fell in front of the Lakeland Fells, Calf Top (Middleton Fell), the Howgill Fells, Crag Hill, Great Coum, Green Hill, High Seat, Lunds Fell, Great Shunner Fell, Widdale Fell, Whernside, Plover Hill, Penyghent, Fountains Fell, Simon Fell and Ingleborough.

To return, retrace steps to the wall and over the stile, but as you approach the steeper edge consider a more interesting route to remain high above Turbary Pasture. Turn left (north) along the crest of the steeper drop, declining only gently to approach a gritstone bouldery rift at the end, just before a descending wall. The location of Yordas Cave in its clump of trees is evident far below. A short, steep section of descent takes you beneath the rocks to follow the wall away. Soon encountering Yordas Gill, slant right across the moor with it to drop to a wall below: follow this right to return to the gate from early in the climb, and drop back down as you began.

Whernside from Gragareth

*4½ miles
from Cowan Bridge*

**The lovely environs of
Leck Beck penetrate
unfrequented fell country**

Start Village centre (GR: 635764),
car park up side road behind shop
Map OS Explorer OL2, Yorkshire Dales South/West
Access Open Access (detour only), see page 5

     Cowan Bridge is a tiny village astride a busy main road. It boasts a shop, Methodist chapel and two old boundary stones. The old bridge itself is sidelined by a modern replacement: alongside is a former Clergymen's Daughters School attended by four of the Bronte sisters in 1824-25. From the main road bridge over Leck Beck, take a stile on the village side and head upstream to pass under an arch of a low viaduct. The former Clapham-Tebay line ran via the Lune Valley and Sedbergh to the main line at the Lune Gorge. Across the field behind it a wall-stile puts you into the beck's environs. A path runs on the edge of the tree-lined bank, a pleasant amble which, if you miss the turn-off, will lead along to a gate to join the adjacent road. The right of way turn off earlier, where a gate/stile send a track along a fieldside towards the first farm buildings, but joining a back road via a stile just before them. Turn left along this and, keeping left at a junction follow it to its demise at the handful of buildings at what was Leck Mill.

     Forking into driveways take the left one, past the house and on to a gate/stile into a field. A cart track heads away through this and a longer field, running along to enter a wood alongside Leck Beck. Emerging, the track runs delightfully on through an extremely long pasture, passing a wooden cabin before reaching a gate/stile at the end. Entering Open Access land, a path traces the beck upstream in very colourful and quite wild country. Though your onward route vacates the beck at the first inflowing stream, a thin path remains with the beck to witness its finest moment a little further: rounding a slabby corner beneath trees you come upon a wonderful gorge containing modest but charming waterfalls.

The right of way, meanwhile, climbs a distinct green way then forks more thinly right to a step-stile into new plantings and up to another out onto a track. Turn right, soon running a decent course along the flank well above older plantations. Fading amid moist, reedy moments, keep on to a ladder-stile at the very end. Your way will now simply shadow the right-hand wall all the way back to Leck Mill. Through a second ladder-stile you enter fields, and a gentle descent starts. Big views ahead look to the Bowland moors beyond the Wenning Valley, while grassy banks and ditches on your left indicate an ancient settlement on Castle Hill. From a stile in the corner continue down to a gate, and with Leck Mill appearing ahead, down to a stream crossing on the valley floor. Ignore a stile in the wall and go on through another gate, then head away to a stone slab crossing of a dry ditch pointing to a corner stile. Resume to the end of the field where a gate puts you back onto the outward route at Leck Mill. If not retracing steps, the quickest return takes the left fork in the road, rising to a crossroads and then turning right - with Leck church spire just to the left - down to the main road.

In the upper reaches of Leck Beck

3¹⁄₄ miles
from Kirkby Lonsdale

**Easy rambling to an
attractive village**

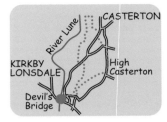

Start Devil's Bridge
(GR: 615782), on edge
of town, car park
Map OS Explorer OL2, Yorkshire Dales South/West

Devil's Bridge is Kirkby Lonsdale's best-known landmark,
its three tall, 15th century arches spanning a lively reach of the Lune:
a refreshment van and WCs do brisk trade. From the east side cross
the Sedbergh road and along a section of old road. At the end it
swings right to the main road, but turn left up a narrow lane. As it
winds up take a kissing-gate on the left into a caravan site. Slant
up to a site road in front of the shop: pass right and a few yards
along another site road before branching right over a cattle-grid.
Turn left on a hedgerowed bridleway, Laitha Lane, swinging right at
the end to a junction. Go left on a firmer course past Casterton
golf course onto the A683: just to the right is a former tollhouse.

Cross to a verge and go cautiously left before escaping
at a kissing-gate on the right. Cross to a fence and double back
right with it towards Casterton Hall: a kissing-gate to its right puts
you onto the drive. Go briefly right to a junction, then double back
left on another drive above wooded grounds. This drops to Mill Hill
House: don't enter but go right to a kissing-gate into a field. Follow
the wood edge away, at the end taking a kissing-gate into the trees.
A broad track goes right above a wooded gill, and as it merges into
a firmer drive, turn off left to bridge the stream. A path heads
away through trees to a stile at the other side, then crosses open
pasture to one back into trees. Another clear path heads away to a
kissing-gate into a field corner. Turn right outside the wood, and
right on to the end in front of an impressive house, The Grange.
Beyond rise Middleton Fell, Barbon Low Fell and Casterton Fell.

Turn right through two gates outside the grounds, and away with a wall on your left, becoming hollowed down to cross a pond outflow to a gate. Rise to a barn and a hedge leads on between sports fields to a driveway at part of Casterton school. Cross over, down into a yard and down steps to a lower yard. Cross the drive behind to a snicket rising between gardens onto the main road in Casterton. Casterton is dominated by its girls' school, established in 1833: the Holy Trinity church was built at the same time. Cross and follow a footway right past a small green and the Pheasant Inn to Town End garage/shop. A stile on the left after it sends an enclosed path past gardens to a kissing-gate into a field. Bear left to a stile in a hedge and maintain that line through another and on to a kissing-gate onto a back road. Go briefly left to a crossroads, then right.

Remain on this past some prestigious dwellings at High Casterton to reach a hamlet where turn right on a dead-end road. This leads past several houses to become an enclosed grassy track, dropping pleasantly between hedgerows to a bend. With the golf course on your right take a stile on the left and rise to the brow of the field. The walk's finest viewpoint features Bowland, Hutton Roof Crags, Kirkby Lonsdale, Underley Hall, the Howgill Fells, Middleton Fell and Casterton Fell. Maintain the slant down to a corner stile, and descend to a kissing-gate into a log cabin enclosure, where a stile puts you back onto Laitha Lane. Go left and remain on the bridleway to a junction at the caravan site entrance. Turn right down the narrow side lane which is the one on which you began.

The Devil's Bridge, Kirkby Lonsdale

4¹⁄₂ miles from Barbon

Quiet lanes lead to the banks of the River Lune, returning via a lively beck

Start Village centre (GR: 628825), car park at village hall
Map OS Explorer OL2, Yorkshire Dales South/West

BARBON

Beckfoot

River Lune

Underley Hall

For a note on Barbon see page 40. From the war memorial leave the village along a side road past the shop and village hall, to where it bends right at Town End. Here take a side road left, but within yards take a stile on the right after a house and head away to another left of a house across the field. Head away in the same direction to a gate ahead, then bear gently right, rising to merge with a hedge: further along is a gap-stile onto a road where a wall takes over. Double back right a short way to a junction, then go left to a crossroads with the A683. Cross and head along Scaleber Lane past the golf club. Where it bends sharp left at a farm road junction, you will return to this point after the Lune loop. Go left past cottages at Low Beckfoot and under a bridge carrying an old driveway to Underley Hall to reach another sharp bend left.

This time take some steps on the right, and a path runs through trees above a solitary house and down to a stile into a big parkland tract. Go left with the fence enclosing the wood until crossing a small watercourse, then bear right to merge with a track alongside a fence, with the wide-flowing River Lune just across it. Bear right to reach a massive, ornate stone-arched bridge carrying the old driveway. This gaunt pile hides in trees over the river: built in the 1820s for the Earl of Bective, it is now a school. Over to the right Middleton Fell, Barbon Low Fell and Casterton Fell form a high skyline. Resume beyond the bridge, and a step-stile further along puts you onto the true riverbank, with a ladder-stile beyond. A grand little path now provides the finest section until beneath overhead power lines, where you reach the site of a ford. Ignoring a ladder-stile just behind, take a gate on the right and head away from the river. When the accompanying fence bends off, cross the field to the right of Low Beckfoot cottages. Joining another drive go left on this out onto the previous road.

Go left past the cottages to the junction, this time taking the unsigned branch straight ahead. This runs to cross lively Barbon Beck at High Beckfoot: alongside is a charming 17th century arched packhorse bridge. Fork right into the yard at Beckfoot Farm, and pass the house to a gate. A gentle track heads upstream through colourful surroundings, soon opening out and fading. Remain near the beck to a stile at the far end, where a path rises onto a golf course. Advance to a plantation ahead and follow its right side, just past the end of which an old, enclosed bridleway is met. Turn right on this to reach the beck again. Whilst bridleway users must ford it, your route simply resumes upstream, still along the edge of the course and concluding with a short stroll to a wall-stile left of a gate ahead. This puts you onto the A683, turn right to cross Hodge Bridge, noting the old stone guidepost at the corner. With Barbon Beck for company, turn along the side road into the village.

Barbon church

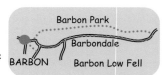

4¹4 miles from Barbon

A charming beck leads through woodland onto the base of open fellside

Barbon Park
Barbondale
BARBON
Barbon Low Fell

Start Village centre (GR: 628825), car park at village hall
Map OS Explorer OL2, Yorkshire Dales South/West

The unassuming village of Barbon nestles in a fine Lune Valley setting, tucked away at the foot of the Dales' westernmost fells. In spite of its enviable location it is virtually a tourist-free area: old Westmorland still lingers on here. Its features include St Bartholomew's church of 1893, the homely Barbon Inn, a Post office/shop, an old Wesleyan chapel and a former reading room of

1884. Centrepiece is the war memorial on which the Shuttleworths of Barbon Manor feature prominently. A narrow road squeezes through the hills to emerge into the heart of Dentdale.

From the memorial leave the village by the road past the pub and the church, turning left along the drive into Barbon Park. Across the bridge on Barbon Beck the drive swings right to climb to Barbon Manor (built in 1863 as a shooting lodge for Sir James Kay-Shuttleworth), but when it swings sharp left away from the beck's wooded environs, a sign indicates a green track heading right to a gate into trees. Lively Barbon Beck is followed all the way through deep woodland, enjoying beck scenery of the highest order. A big stone-arched bridge is reached where a broader track is met. Bear left on this, rising away from the beck and on to a gate out of the trees. The splendid track runs a grand course through bracken along the base of the steep fell, with the beck below and Barbon Low Fell across it: ahead is the high wall of Crag Hill. At the end, beyond an intervening gate, is a pair of gates alongside a sheepfold. This is a lovely spot, looking over the confluence of Aygill with Barbon Beck amid tilted rocks.

Just a little further, a footbridge conveys you to the Dentdale road on the other side, opposite Fell House farm drive. Turn right with the beck, then rising to crossing Aygill at Blindbeck Bridge. Now simply remain on this unfenced road along the base of the fell, taking advantage of some good verges. After more than a mile a fork is reached: keep right, down over a cattle-grid to drop back towards the village, which is revealed only at the last moment.

When it does appear, at a minor side road, conclude by turning briefly left on this grass stripped lane, then quickly right down a bridleway (Watery Lane), draped in dense greenery. At the bottom it bridges the former railway line and runs as a green way down onto an access road. Just ahead is a junction with a through road, turning right into the centre.

The Lunesdale Hunt heading for Barbon Low Fell
Left: War memorial, Barbon

*4¹4 miles
from Barbon*

**Superb Dales scenery in
an unfrequented corner**

*Start Dentdale road
(GR: 637824), lay-by at cattle-grid, ³4 miles out of village
Map OS Explorer OL2, Yorkshire Dales South/West
Access Open Access, see page 5*

Above the parking area is a junction at the foot of
Barbon Low Fell: go left on the Dentdale road, with good verges for
a long mile above initially wooded Barbondale. A hundred yards
before dropping to cross Aygill at Blindbeck Bridge, take a green
way slanting right. This climb offers fine views north to Middleton
Fell's long wall. The old way scales the lower contours of Barbon Low
Fell, absorbing another track to ease on gentler ground. Gragareth's
long skyline appears ahead, and the track runs to a gate where it
becomes enclosed. Just prior to this, colourful Aygill ravine is just
through a gate/stile on the left. Your onward route doesn't go
through onto the lane, which offers a detour to Bullpot Farm, a
caving club base for some of our finest cave systems. Beyond the
house a wallside path runs to Bull Pot of the Witches, a forbidding
hole dropping some 200ft/60m: wet spells see a waterfall pouring
over the lip, though it is easier to hear than see, in safety.

Without passing through the gate turn up the near side
of the wall to remain on open fell. Ascend this grassy slope largely
with the wall, intermittent sheeptrods easing progress. Beneath
telegraph wires you rise to a knoll, then on again with a stony edge
over to the right. Another minor knoll is gained to earn big views
ahead. The various knolls of Barbon Low Fell and adjoining Casterton
Fell are foreground to a distant panorama of the Lakeland Fells. A
tiny descent sends you off again, a fairly level meander on trods to
rise to the walk's highest point at some 1410ft/430m on a welcoming

green knoll just up from the wall. This splendid viewpoint features Bowland, Casterton Fell, Morecambe Bay, Hutton Roof Crags, Farleton Fell, the Lakeland Fells across the Lune Valley, Whinfell, Middleton Fell, Barbondale, Baugh Fell, Rise Hill, Crag Hill, Gragareth.

Resume and descend close by the wall, neatly evading the large Nanslope Moss and then on to a minor knoll. This overlooks a more appreciable drop to a hollow. Descend pleasant slopes then follow a trod (keeping away from the wall) along a gentle ridge to approach a wall junction. Casterton Fell is richly carpeted with heather over the wall ahead. Swing right with the wall, on a thin trod shadowing it round two bends to neatly avoid a marsh. Striding the outflow at a tidy confluence, just ahead a fence replaces the wall and the stream transforms into a broadening ravine.

This good little path traces it down steeper slopes, fading in bracken at the bottom. Pass a large old sheepfold and down to a smaller one across the tiny beck. Behind the fold a grass track runs left through bracken, shadowing the little stream then bearing right and fading a little on grass. Below is the big house of Whelprigg, while Lune Valley views soon open out. Swinging right away from the main beck the track quickly re-forms in bracken, and slants as a super green way down bracken fellside to an unfenced road on the base of the fell. Turn right, taking advantage of verges to return to the start. Round a slight bend Barbon Manor (1863) appears in trees ahead.

Middleton Fell from above Aygill

4 miles from Old Town

Easy walking on old tracks and byways in an unsung corner, enjoying extensive views across to the Lunesdale fells

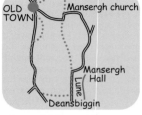

Start Hamlet centre
(GR: 595829), on B6254
Kirkby Lonsdale-Kendal road, roadside parking
Map OS Explorer OL2, Yorkshire Dales South/West

Though no more than a hamlet, Old Town is the centre of the scattered parish of Mansergh, pronounced 'Manser'. It enjoys views across the Lune Valley to the Howgill Fells, Middleton Fell, Great Coum and Casterton Fell. Head south on the road, passing the old village pump. Beyond the last house it rises away, but before the brow take a stile on the left. Through this descend the wallside, at the bottom corner bearing right with it to slant down to a fence-stile and then a gate onto a track serving the chalets of Lune Valley Park. Cross the grassed area opposite to a stile in front of Hawkrigg farmhouse, and turn right through the yard.

At the end advance straight on through a gate and along a hedgerowed track, transforming into a grassy bridleway. This runs pleasantly along to emerge back onto the B6254, where turn left. Shortly after Deansbiggin Tram Plantation starts, note an old milestone on the right: '10' and '2' refer to mileages to Kendal and Kirkby Lonsdale. Just 120 yards beyond a junction the true right of way goes left through a gap in the beech hedge, but its crossing of part wooded and bracken terrain is blocked: better to trace a path parallel with the road to a drive just a little further. Turn left down this to the farm of Deansbiggin, keeping left of the house. Remain on the firm track past some barns before descending a hedgerowed course onto a road. During this the view to Barbon and Casterton Fells expands to include Middleton Fell and the Howgill Fells.

Go left for a few minutes to approach Mansergh Hall, with a farm shop and a backdrop of fells. Level with its drive bear left up an enclosed cart track, Chapel Lane. This rises to run a grand course, with Old Town to the left and Mansergh church ahead. At the end a gate puts you into a field. The eastern panorama reaches from the Howgill Fells all the way back to Bowland. Continue with an old hedge on your left to a gate at the end. The faint way then crosses a field centre to a gate onto St Peter's church driveway. Dating from 1880 it occupies an enviable if isolated setting. Advance on to the road just ahead alongside the former school of 1839.

Go right on the narrow road, and at a sharp bend right, bear left up an enclosed track: while this quickly enters a field, a super hedgerowed bridleway rises gently towards a brow. From a squeezer-stile on the left follow a wall away to rise outside a tiny wood. Continue on with the wall through a gate, and just before the corner beyond take a stile in the wall and follow the hedge away.

Your final panorama now embraces Middleton Fell, Crag Hill, Barbon Low Fell, Casterton Fell and a long Bowland skyline along to Clougha Pike. When the hedge ends bear right down the field to locate a wall-stile between a gate and the field corner. Turn right to a gate in the wall ahead, and cross the field to a stile at the house at Greenbank. Advance on the lawned enclosure to a stile onto a back road. The main road through Old Town is just a minute to the left. At the junction is an old milestone inscribed 'Kirkby Lonsdale 3, Kendal 9', with the inclusion of the 253 miles to London.

Mansergh church

*4¹4 miles
from Rigmaden*

**Exploring the scattered
parish of Middleton by
fields, farms and lanes**

*Start Rigmaden Bridge
(GR: 617848), on Old Town road
off Kirkby Lonsdale-Sedbergh road, parking on east side
Map OS Explorer OL2, Yorkshire Dales South/West*

Rigmaden Bridge is the only crossing of the Lune between Killington and Kirkby Lonsdale, and gives a lovely view of the river backed by the Howgill Fells. Don't cross but head east towards the main road. As the wooded bank ends, Middleton Fell is revealed ahead. Just before the main road go left on the hedgerowed, grassy track of Low Lane, broadening to lead to a farm road. Go left on this to Hawking Hall, and entering the yard bear right to a corner gate. A rough track heads off beneath a wooded bank, with Middleton church visible ahead. When the bank ends the distinctive pillar of a Roman milestone is seen on the brow ahead: unearthed in 1836 and neatly cylindrical, it rises to almost six feet. Your route crosses the flat field to the right-hand gate in a fence opposite, then bears right to a gate/stile right of the church. Joining the main road go left to Middleton's isolated church of the Holy Ghost, dating from 1879.

Continue a short while further, past an old milestone with distances to Sedbergh and Kirkby Lonsdale. Just beyond it go right on a narrow lane: one minute further on the main road is the Swan Inn. The lane runs to a junction at High Stockdale Bridge. Turn briefly right, and when it swings sharp right take a stile on the left. Rise across the field to a corner gate, then cross to one into Ullathorns farmyard. Noting the house with its 1617 datestone, turn right on the drive. When it swings right to the road, take a gate in front and head off on the wallside, through another gate and on to a corner, where slant left up to Tossbeck. From a gate into the yard, turn

46

left between the buildings to an underpass beneath the Clapham-Lowgill railway, closed in 1964.

Rising into a field, bear right along the bottom edge to a stile onto an access road. From one opposite slant left to a stile in a tumbledown wall, then on to a corner gate in a dip. A stile just behind sees you maintain this line, rising to a hidden stile in a corner just ahead. Slant up a bigger field to a gate in the fence above, just yards short of the corner, then on again to a stile onto a surfaced access road. Rise left to Mill House, through a gate to cottages above. From a stile between them a little path drops to bridge Millhouse Beck. Continue to a barn ahead then bear right, briefly, down a stony track to a gateway in the wall beneath a traditional old barn.

From the gateway cross a large pasture to approach Low Fellside: towards the end is a wall-stile in line with the house. Go left of the house to a corner gate above outbuildings. Continue past a barn and down to a small gate in a fence ahead. Drop right to a gate just below, then rise away with the fence on your right, dropping to a stile and along to another at the end. From one behind it you run down to a stile onto a railway cutting. Cross and resume down to a stile onto a back road. Turn right and immediately fork left, then a minute later take a gate/stile on the left. Cross the long field centre to a stile, and continue with a hedge, dropping through a stile and on to one onto the main road junction. With the big house of Rigmaden Park ahead over the valley, cross straight over to finish.

The Lune at Rigmaden Bridge

HILLSIDE GUIDES... cover much of Northern England

Other colour *Pocket Walks* guides (more in preparation)
·UPPER WHARFEDALE ·LOWER WHARFEDALE
·UPPER WENSLEYDALE ·LOWER WENSLEYDALE
·MALHAMDALE ·SWALEDALE ·RIBBLESDALE
·INGLETON/WESTERN DALES ·SEDBERGH/DENTDALE
·NIDDERDALE ·HARROGATE/KNARESBOROUGH
·BOWLAND ·AROUND PENDLE ·RIBBLE VALLEY
·AMBLESIDE/LANGDALE ·BORROWDALE
·AIRE VALLEY ·ILKLEY/WASHBURN VALLEY

Our *Walking Country* range features more great walks...

·WHARFEDALE ·MALHAMDALE ·WENSLEYDALE
·HARROGATE & the WHARFE VALLEY ·SWALEDALE
·RIPON & LOWER WENSLEYDALE ·NIDDERDALE
·THREE PEAKS ·HOWGILL FELLS ·HOWARDIAN HILLS
·TEESDALE ·EDEN VALLEY ·ALSTON & ALLENDALE

·ILKLEY MOOR ·BRONTE COUNTRY ·CALDERDALE
·PENDLE & the RIBBLE ·WEST PENNINE MOORS
·ARNSIDE & SILVERDALE ·LUNESDALE ·BOWLAND

·LAKELAND FELLS, SOUTH ·LAKELAND FELLS, EAST
·LAKELAND FELLS, NORTH ·LAKELAND FELLS, WEST

Long Distance Walks
·COAST TO COAST WALK ·CUMBRIA WAY ·DALES WAY
·LADY ANNE'S WAY ·NIDDERDALE WAY
·WESTMORLAND WAY ·FURNESS WAY
·PENDLE WAY ·BRONTE WAY ·CALDERDALE WAY

Visit www.hillsidepublications.co.uk
or write for a catalogue